The Disappearance of Jessie Foster

Annie Sims

Published by Trellis Publishing, 2021.

THE DISAPPEARANCE OF JESSIE FOSTER

First edition. July 3, 2021.

Copyright © 2021 Annie Sims.

ISBN: 979-8224763146

Written by Annie Sims.

THE DISAPPEARANCE OF JESSIE FOSTER

ANNIE SIMS

Disappearance of Jessie Foster

Like so many cases of missing people, the story of Jessie Foster has not ended, either happily or otherwise. Jessie Foster has been missing since 2006 and her sudden disappearance has people raising more questions than the world can answer. Many people point to her past and her shady companions, while other blame the mysterious city of Las Vegas for her missing status. Whatever the case, there leads that have been followed have all ended in dead ends.

Jessie Foster was born on May 27, 1984, to Glendene Grant and Dwight Foster. They lived in Canada and spent a lot of their time in Calgary, Alberta. Jessie herself spent most of her teen- and adult-life living in Kamloops, British Columbia. Little has been said about her personality, career, and educational level. All we know is that she was a popular athlete and an honor roll student prior to disappearing.

Jessie became missing officially in 2006 after living in Las Vegas for a little while. However, like any missing persons' case, sometimes the most important pieces of information are hidden in the days, months and even years prior to disappearing. In Jessie's case, things did appear strange to family members and friends who were silently watching over her.

When Jessie moved back to Kamloops, British Columbia, she soon got back in contact with a close friend from high school: Donald Vaz. Not long after settling in to Kamloops, Vaz invited Jessie to come with him to Fort Lauderdale, Florida, to meet his mother for unexplained reasons. This was odd because his mother was living in Edmonton, Alberta, at the time.

In early 2005, Dwight would constantly suggest to his daughter to relax and take time off of her busy work schedule to travel. Jessie would initially brush these suggestions away with reasons for meeting deadlines or having too much work to do. However, she finally relented and became much more open to the suggestion of traveling the world. Vaz's invitation to see Florida was an excellent place to start, and she found no reason to reject.

It was in Jessie's nature to be trusting of people; that's one of the things that her parents usually faulted her for. When her friend asked her to accompany him to Florida, she didn't hesitate to accept the invitation. Not everyday do you have a reason to go to the warm south to escape chilly Canada, even if it's just for a couple weeks. And it's even rarer that you get the chance to travel for free since Vaz offered to pay for tickets, lodging, and food.

Jessie just brought her necessities with her and hopped onto the plane headed for Fort Lauderdale. After they returned to Canada, Jessie stayed for a little while in Kamloops before Vaz invited her to take a second trip to Manhattan, New York. After being offered a second trip by her high school friend to another country, this should've been the first warning sign for Jessie. However, her overly trusting nature told her to go to Vaz and see the Big Apple.

From New York, they went to Atlantic City, New Jersey. However, there was a fight between the high school friends which put a delay on their plans to return home. During their stay in New Jersey, she contacted both her mother and father (separated at the time) and told them of her situation and how she would handle it. Both her parents told retold phone conversations with Jessie with significant discrepancies.

Glendene – Jassie's mother – recalled the conversation she had with her daughter when they were stranded in New Jersey. "Jessie told me that her and Donald had a fight in their hotel room because she had lost all his money gambling and he wanted her to prostitute herself so he can get some money."

Glendene offered to pay for her trip home via Ontario. "She called me later and said everything was fine and then she called me the next day to say she was going to come home via Las Vegas instead of Toronto. She said her 21st birthday was in two weeks and she wanted to go visit her friend, Yvonne in Las Vegas and perhaps stay there for her birthday."

It's very common for new 21-year olds from Canada to visit Las Vegas to spend their birthdays so to Glendene nothing was out of the ordinary. Although disappointed that she remained with Vaz through the whole ordeal, she was glad that her daughter had everything planned out. However, one detail of their trip was either intentionally unmentioned during her phone conversations with her mom. "She told me she did NOT go to Atlantic City, New Jersey, on this trip." Jessie retold the story to her sister, Crystal, and basically said the same things she told her mom, except she mentioned that they did in fact go to New Jersey.

The version she told her father, Dwight, had different details in comparison to Glendene's and Crystal's versions. "She told me that her friend lost all his money gambling," Dwight recalls from his conversation with Jessie during her trip to New York and New Jersey, "and that he wanted me to 'turn a few tricks' to earn some money so they could get out of the USA and back to Canada. Jessie got mad and left the room, going to the hotel lobby and called me."

The three versions have differences in details, and so far there's no reason why she would give different accounts of the same story to three people. This is most likely the most complete information of her details with Vaz during their trip to New York, maybe New Jersey, and ultimately Nevada.

Jessie and Vaz arrived at Las Vegas, Nevada, on May 13, 2006. They soon met up with her friend, Yvonne (aka Angel), and would spend a couple nights at her place in preparation for Jessie's birthday. Her parents weren't entirely excited about the prospect of their daughter spending so much time away from home, especially after her whole argument with Vaz whom her parents were not on great terms with. Her parents requested Yvonne's phone number so they could have the contact of somebody there in case anything bad happened to Jessie.

Yvonne was a known prostitute and was previously charged with attempting to transport a minor across state borders for sexual purposes. She was also well-known in Vancouver, British Columbia, as a person who would frequent the red light districts in search of her next victim to smuggle out. Because of her shady past and obvious lack of guilt, she was deported from the country.

It should be apparent now Jessie's acquaintances aren't exactly the best of people. One tried to persuade her to prostitute herself in order to make cash to return home, and the other was known for smuggling minors past state lines. It was only a matter of time before something bad happened to Jessie, and that precise moment was coming quickly.

Peter Todd became Jessie's boyfriend during her stay in Las Vegas. Todd was the friend of Yvonne's boyfriend who was quickly introduced to Jessie. Not long after knowing each other, Jessie moved in with Todd. Jessie was to stay with Todd until her birthday where, according to their planes, they would spend the day drinking, gambling. Basically, they'd spend the whole day in a Las Vegas casino doing regular party-people things.

After weeks of knowing Todd and living in his lavish home, Jessie's parents received news that their daughter was now in police custody and was charged for prostitution. Her parents were dumbfounded by the news and thought it was impossible that someone with such a clean track record in her personal and academic life would be caught doing something so strange. Their first guess was that Todd somehow made Jessie become a prostitute, either by force or by tricking her. Jessie went to court and paid a fine of $600 since it was her first offense.

Todd was there are her hearing and paid the fine before quickly sweeping her away into his car and bringing her back home. The things that Glendene read and heard about in Las Vegas around the time her daughter moved there were worrying. "There is another woman named Lindsay Marie Harris," Glendene writes in her blog, "who went missing in May 2006, just two months before [Jessie] arrived in Las Vegas. Did they replace Lindsay with Jessie?"

According to some reports, Jessie and Lindsay had the same description, upbringing, and missing person story. In addition, Lindsay was arrested five times before suddenly vanishing into thin air. "Were

Lindsay and Jessie bumped?" Glendene asks herself and her blog reader. "Were they determined to be more trouble than they were worth, to their pimps or human traffickers?" Some speculate that Lindsay and Jessie were both discovered by the same people and pushed into sex trafficking before being forcibly removed.

Glendene called Lindsay's parents, wanting to talk about the similarities between the stories of their missing daughters but only reached their voicemail. They returned the call back to Glendene and told her everything they knew about the case. At the time, Lindsay was missing for about a year and like Jessie, the North Las Vegas Police Department hardly had any leads to follow.

"[Lidnsay's mother] knew her daughter was not alive," Glendene recalls in her blog about her missing daughter, "She has never felt that Lindsay is alive. And, sadly, neither did Lindsay's twin brother." After three years, Glende heard news of Lindsay's body being found by police. Lindsay's and Jessie's DNA were compared against a body found by the police department. "She knew she wasn't alive, and she was right. The police have told me it is sometimes their best investigative tool... mother."

After several months of their relationship, Jessie and her boyfriend were engaged to get married. The whole time she was in Las Vegas, she would keep her family updated on her situation. "She would call me and Jim – her stepdad – several times a week. Same with her dad and Tracy – her stepmother. Her sisters and friends got calls and text messages several times a week but sometimes [even] several times a day."

During her ten month stay in Las Vegas, she only returned to Canada once to see her family. "It was only for a few weeks at the end of the year 2005, and we even though – hoped – she might stay in Canada, since she and Peter, her fiancé in North Las Vegas, Nevada, was now a known pimp and the person known to the police on Jessie's case." In her frequent calls to her fiancé while she was back in Canada, Jessie and Todd would argue endlessly over the phone.

"I was actually happy since it seemed they always fought," Glendene says in her blog about her missing daughter, "and now she was home and did not have to put up with it." Jessie would talk to her mother over the phone during her arguments with her fiancé, and Glendene even pleaded to Todd to let her daughter return home safely. "They would always make up and she never came home to live."

On Christmas day in 2005, Jessie was to return to Las Vegas and Todd to resume her life there. "Jessie told us we needed to drive her to the airport because she had to get back to Las Vegas to see [Todd]. It was so urgent and out of the blue, we tried to find out what was going on. She said nothing."

The following months after New Year's were pretty much repetitive for the newly engaged couple: they'd argue, Jessie would call her mom or dad, they'd make up, and everything would be fine until the next argument. There is little information on what occurred during the months after her return to Las Vegas after Christmas 2005. However, things would suddenly become a parent's worst nightmare when, out of nowhere, Jessie went missing.

The last reported sighting of Jessie was of her exiting the premises of her fiancé's home with her bags in her arms, apparently packed up and ready to go. There was no sighting of Todd, and there is speculation that the couple's constant bickering finally forced Jessie to take matters into her own hands and leave.

After this occurrence, Jessie went missing the North Las Vegas Police Department reported finding three other women. All of them, including Jessie herself, were known prostitutes living and working in North Las Vegas. As soon as the bodies were found, the police launched an immediate investigation to find the killer or anyone involved in the killing of the three women.

After discovering that their daughter was missing, Glendene and Dwight automatically pointed fingers at Todd as the person to blame for their missing daughter. The police took Todd into custody and interrogated him regarding Jessie's whereabouts and what the magnitude of their relationship was. Surprisingly, Todd was clean and had seemingly had no reason to cause harm on his fiancé. The police let him go but felt compelled to interrogate him again after a clue in Jessie's missing case brought them back to Todd. The police searched his home and his belongings but nothing was found that could pin Todd as a responsible party for her disappearance. Again, the police released him and he was no longer a suspect.

After three years of grasping at straws, Glendene and Dwight are unable to blame Todd, Vaz, or even Yvonne on their missing daughter. Things were suspicious from the start, especially with Vaz who took their daughter to Fort Lauderdale, Florida, under false pretenses of meeting his mother. There was absolutely no reason for him to lie to Jessie, seeing as how she would've traveled with an old high school friend to sunny Floridian beaches in a heartbeat.

Yvonne, the friend living is Las Vegas who was charged with selling a minor for sex purposes, is another shady character that, for reasons unknown, managed to befriend Jessie and maintain that relationship long enough that Jessie would come to Las Vegas and stay with her in preparation for her birthday. Even knowing her dubious past, Jessie could still trust her enough to live with her and meet her mutual friends. This leads to Peter Todd who was the last person to ever have a significant relationship with Jessie before leaving.

What hold did Todd have on Jessie that made her absolutely have to leave for Las Vegas during Christmas day 2005? Was she deeply in love with Todd that she was his puppet? Was he threatening her over the phone to do something to her if she didn't return? Was Jessie's family threatened? Why are Glendene and Dwight so sure that Todd is involved in making their daughter disappear when even the police can't find any evidence that would suspect him of any wrongdoing?

Ever since Jessie disappeared that day in Las Vegas, the course of Glendene's and Dwight's lives changed. There's nothing more devastating to a parent than losing a child and not knowing what happened to them. They're not a part of the what-ifs and body watches community. They get on the edge of their seats whenever the remains of a person are discovered.

In the beginning, both her parents were constantly stressed about what possible torture their daughter would be going through. The mystery of their missing daughter was like an open wound that wouldn't heal. The continuous train of thought about any and every possible bad thing to happen to their daughter had crossed their mind.

During the first year of Jessie's disappearance, Glendene refused to leave her house and even allowed her food stock to run dry several times. She was constantly grieving over the loss of her daughter whilst raising the daughters who remained in Canada. She left her job and dedicated her time and resources into finding what happened to her beloved daughter who left for Las Vegas so many years ago.

Both Glendene and Dwight hired a private investigator that frequently traveled to Las Vegas to search the entire city for their daughter. Unfortunately, the private investigator found nothing – no clues, no rumors, no ideas, and no Jessie. It seemed as if everything that could go wrong went wrong. However, the private investigator did uncover some historical information regarding their daughter that they were unaware of before. Apparently, Jessie had been hospitalized with a broken jaw and arrested twice for prostitution.

Then, near the end of the first year of Jessie's disappearance, Glendene received a signal that caused her to continue her search for Jessie. While on a flight to Las Vegas to do some of her own personal searching, she learned that police in Missouri had found Sean Hornsbeck – a child who was kidnapped – after four years of searching. Though four years was still much too long for Glendene to wait, it was better than nothing. She grasped onto that ray of hope and set a goal of finding her daughter within the first four years of her search.

However, it's been 11 years now and no new leads have surfaced that could unite Glendene and Dwight with their missing daughter. In 2015, there were reports that a man found dead in Oregon could possibly be linked to what happened to Jessie so many years ago. The man succumbed to fatal gunshot wounds when a prostitute pulled the trigger in self defense. The man was being investigated to ties with several unsolved cases including prostitutes, and even one that involves a Calgary woman.

"I do believe Jessie is alive," Glendene told reporters after hearing of the Oregon man's ill fate, "But I want answers, and not only the ones I wanted. I will accept what happened to Jessie and I will go on. If this is what [the Oregon man] was doing 10 years ago, there is a possibility... [If Jessie's dead], it is more likely this type of person did something to her." Dwight never commented on the case of the murdered man from Oregon, mainly due to his deep depression stemming from his missing daughter.

"The dark thoughts come in – you close your eyes for a few minutes – and your thoughts invariably go to my daughter," he told reporters in a previous interview, "I don't even want to think about it because those are thoughts that rip you to pieces."

The only information available about Jessie in Las Vegas are depressing and causes Glendene to become less hopeful of her daughter's return. Jessie's hospital records suggest that she was involved with a ring of violent people in Las Vegas. The subsequent reports of Jessie's involvement in prostitution were like fitting two pieces of a puzzle together. "It's like all of a sudden I realized, taken to another country, beaten and forced into the sex trade – yeah, that's exactly what that is." Meanwhile, Dwight believes that his daughter – a highly ambitious person with deep love for money and the good life – may have willingly entered the profession in order to fulfill any new addictions she picked up in Las Vegas.

11 years later, without any idea about the whereabouts of their missing daughter, Glendene and Dwight still dwell on this mysterious missing persons case. However, they both have different ways of dealing with the depression and psychological scars.

Dwight mainly holds onto the issue himself and rarely speaks of his daughter out of fear of reopening emotional wounds. He's still living with his family, but at times he can seem distant and unwilling to socialize. He spends his nights awake in his study, constantly thinking and reminiscing of his missing daughter. He's no longer the happy guitar-playing father he was before the incident that caused his daughter to leave his life. A father who's missing a daughter with whom he was extremely close to can easily close himself off from the outside world.

Meanwhile, Glendene has taken another approach of dealing with her depression. Instead of staying indoors and out of sight, she started Mothers Against Trafficking Humans, a non-profit organization dedicated to helping reunite families suffering from past sex trafficking crimes, in her daughter's name. Glendene has taken it upon herself to dedicate time and money to the cause and feels a vicarious happiness when broken families can become whole again.

Early on in the case, a detective advised Glendene not to try and make this a national issue since "no one would be interested in Jessie's story." Glendene didn't take that sitting down and immediately ran multiple campaigns to raise awareness of the very real, very dangerous problem of human trafficking. Jessie's story has appeared in numerous documentaries, bookies and newspapers. Glendene is also invited to many high schools and universities each year to talk about her missing daughter and speak about sex trafficking.

"I don't lose hope," Glendene said in an interview regarding her missing daughter and the organization she helms, "but I don't dream about the what-ifs. Those are the ones that will put you in the psych ward." When asked about what she thinks of Dwight's coping mechanism, she appears sympathetic. "Somewhere in his dad mind, he probably felt that he didn't protect her."

One day, after 10 years of searching, Glendene was alerted by police that a homeless woman was found intoxicated and had a very slight resemblance to her young 21-year old daughter. Glendene has had her spirits lift to the sky and brought down to hell before, and she knew she shouldn't get her hopes up. But something about the call made her truly believe that the homeless woman might be her daughter.

At around midnight the police were still doing their regular tests on their late-night detainees, and the fingerprint scan results were almost done. In the meantime, Metro Police called Glendene and told her of the situation. Earlier that night, Metro Police found the woman and wouldn't respond to any questions, including their line of questions regarding Jessie Foster. The police took three pictures of the woman and sent them to Glendene.

Looking at the photographs, the first two pictures were not even remotely close to the facial features of her missing daughter. But something in the third picture caused her to remember her daughter and show a positive sign that this homeless woman might very well be the daughter she has fought 11 years to find.

In order to draw a clear conclusion, the police gave the phone to the homeless woman to speak with Glendene. Glendene asked a number of questions but received no response. She became angry with the homelass person for her lack of cooperation and understanding, but the fingerprint scans were complete and conclusive. This woman, who has a very slight resemblance to Jessie Foster in one of her pictures taken by a police offer whilst she was intoxicated, was unequivocally not the Glendene's missing daughter.

"I wanted it to be her," Glendene said hopelessly as she received the report. The heart and soul can only take so much of a pounding before the body decides to retreat into the recesses of a dark, empty room with nothing for company except old pictures and memories. Again, it happened to Glendene and again she has to pick up what remaining hope she has to continue the search for her daughter. The next day, the search for Jessie Foster continued.

If anybody has any information about the possible whereabouts of Jessie Foster (now aged 34) who was last seen in Las Vegas, Nevada, please inform the North Las Vegas Police Department or Calgary Police Force of Alberta. The latest reward offered for any information leading to the successful finding of Jessie Foster was $50,000. A hope-filled mother and depressed father eagerly await the day where their beloved daughter can return to their arms safe and sound, or where they can finally receive the closure they have been in search of since 2006.

MISSING BEAUMONT CHILDREN

It was a warm summer morning on January 26, 1966, when the three Beaumont children left their suburban home to celebrate Australia Day at the beach. The children regularly made the trip by themselves, so their mother felt at ease providing them with bus fare and sending them on their way while she visited and had lunch with a close friend. However, she would return home that afternoon to find that the children still had not returned. That morning would end up being the last time she saw her three children.

Jane (aged 9), Arnna (aged 7), and Grant (aged 4), lived in Somerton Park, a quiet suburb minutes away from Adelaide, South Australia. Their father, Jim Beaumont, was a linen goods salesman who frequently traveled for work and their mother, Nancy Beaumont, was a stay-at-home mother.

The oldest child, Jane, was viewed by her parents as responsible enough to supervise the other children for short trips and adventures, a style of parenting that was the norm in Australia at that time. The children frequently took the five-minute bus ride to neighboring Glenely Beach by themselves and were looking forward to celebrating the national holiday at the beach.

The children left their home at 10:00am that morning and were seen arriving at the beach by witnesses at 10:15am. They spent much of that morning at play on the beach and were supposed to arrive home at 2:00pm. When they did not arrive at the appointed time, their mother assumed that they had become preoccupied with celebrating the holiday with their playmates and that they would arrive on the next bus or had decided to walk home, something that the three children had done before. When the children did not disembark from the next scheduled bus, their mother began to grow worried.

The disappearance of the Beaumont children would result in one of the largest manhunts and police investigations in Australian history. Furthermore, the event had widespread consequences on Australian society, shattering the illusion that many parents had regarding their children's safety and changing the way that Australians parented their children forever.

Timeline of Events

10:00am - The children leave their Somerton Park home to travel to Glenely Beach by bus.

10:15am - They are seen exiting the bus by multiple witnesses.

11:00am - The three children are spotted playing beneath a sprinkler by an elderly woman. A tall blond man is spotted lying on the ground next to them, watching the children play.

11:15am - A tall blond man is seen playing with the children. They all appear to be laughing and at ease.

11:45am - The children purchase several pastries and a meat pie from the beach snack shop.

12:15pm - The tall blond man and the children are seen leaving the beach together. The children are witnessed laughing together and holding hands.

3:00pm - A postman on his route spots the children walking along Jetty Road alone, away from the beach. The postman is known to the children and they exchange greetings. Police believe that the timeline for this event is incorrect.

7:20pm - The parents of the children become gravely concerned and file a missing children's report with the local police department. Jim Beaumont and the local police search the entire Glenely Beach area.

8:40pm - Police search the surrounding beaches with no results. The father contacts friends and relatives in an attempt to locate the children.

10:00pm - Police issue public radio announcements with a missing children report.

Points of Interest

There are several details in this story which raised doubts with both the parents of the children and the local police department. When the children departed for Glenely Beach in the morning of January 26th, they left with only enough money to cover their bus fare: six shilling and a sixpence. However, the shop owner, who sold several pastries and a meat pie to the children at 11:45am, reported that the children paid for the food with a $1 bill, an amount of money that they did not have when they left their mother's care.

In addition, the shop owner knew the children well and had sold them food and pastries several times before. He reported that the children had never purchased a meat pie before. This suggests that the children received the money from someone after leaving their parents home and that they may have been purchasing the meat pie for someone else.

Lastly, the mother of the children, Nancy Beaumont, repeatedly said that her children were quite shy and very unlikely to speak with strangers, indicating that they may have met the tall blond man prior to the date of their disappearance. Their mother also remembered a seemingly innocuous comment from Arnna, who had previously told her mother that Jane had "got a boyfriend down the beach." Nancy assumed that her daughter was referring to a young playmate, but in hindsight it seems that she may have been referring to the tall blond man spotted by witnesses.

Police Investigation

The South Australian police force began investigating the disappearance of the children in full-force the evening of their disappearance. After interviewing several witnesses who were present at Glenely Beach, they were able to determine that the children were playing with a tall blond, "thin-faced" man while at the beach. He was described as being a blond man in his late 30s with a thin or athletic build.

"Things seemed bungled from the get-go," forensic psychologist Paula Orange said. "First off, the artist drawing the picture admitted to being drunk at the time of completing his task. So the sketch made of the suspect looks more like a lantern-jawed alien than a real person. Secondly, the witnesses claimed that the man was in his late thirties. Witnesses are notorious for getting ages wrong and the police dismissed too many possible subjects out of hand because they didn't fit the profile."

Several witnesses stated that the man was seen dressing the children prior to leaving the beach. The children's parents said that the kids, especially Jane, were very shy and unlikely to speak to a stranger. This later led police to theorize that the children had met the man in question prior to the date of their disappearance and had grown to know him over a period of several weeks.

The blond man and three children were seen leaving the beach together at 12:15pm, after the children purchased several pastries and a meat pie from a local vendor with a $1 bill, an amount of money that they did not have when they left their home that morning.

A wrench was thrown into the investigation when a postman, who knew the children and was on friendly terms with them, reported that he saw the children around 3:00pm that afternoon walking away from the beach and in the direction of their home in Somerton Park. He stated that he exchanged greetings with the young children and that they seemed to be in good spirits. In particular, the postman said that he say the children were "holding hands and laughing" as they walked down the road alone, with no blond companion in sight. Police later said that they believed the postman was mistaken about the timeline and that he most likely saw the children walking some time before noon.

Several months later, a woman in a nearby neighborhood contacted police and told them that she had seen a man with two girls and a young boy enter an abandoned house on her street. She also reported seeing the young boy walking away from the house before he was roughly grabbed by, and returned to the house with, the older man. She never saw the man or children again.

"The response from the public was overwhelming," Orange said. "People drove from miles away to aid in the search. They combed the beach and drained part of it all to no avail. They found nothing, not a trace."

The police were quickly able to eliminate drowning as the cause of the children's disappearance as a result of several witnesses saying that they saw the children leave the beach around 12:15pm. Furthermore, all of the children's belongings were missing, lending further support to the theory that they left the beach. After speaking with the parents, the police were able to identify seventeen different items that were carried by the children that day, providing a list of items that could be used to identify their remains or whereabouts. However, the police's continue efforts continued to prove fruitless.

The Psychic Circus

On November 8, 1966, nearly a year after the children's initial disappearance, an internationally-renowned psychic from the Netherlands, Gerard Croiset, was flown to Australia to investigate the case. His presence caused a whirlwind of media coverage in Australia and across the world. After making a series of outlandish and ever-changing claims, Croiset claimed that the children were buried underneath a warehouse just minutes away from the children's school.

"I appreciate him (Gerard Croiset) coming out to find the children," Jim Beaumont said. "But I don't believe what he said. I don't believe the children are dead and will continue to believe until given evidence that proves otherwise."

The building, which was under construction at the time of their disappearance, was eventually razed and excavated after the owners raised $40,000 for the project as a result of public pressure. No evidence of the children or their belongings were ever found.

"The press and police followed Croiset around everywhere," Orange said. "He was an obvious con artist but they were desperate. They had nothing."

A Series of Letters

Beginning in 1968, the parents of the three children began to receive a series of letters which rekindled hope in the idea that their children may still be alive. Postmarked from Dandernong, Victoria, the series of letters claimed to be written by Jane, the eldest daughter. She claimed to be under the supervision of a man and in good health and care, saying

Dear Mum and Dad,

We had a beautiful lunch today...The man is feeding us really well. The man took us to see The Sound of Music yesterday.

Police officers believed the letters to be from Jane after comparing them to examples of her handwriting and, as far as 1981, the Sidney Morning Herald produced analysis from handwriting experts claiming that the letters were actually from the missing child.

Following receipt of the letters supposedly sent from Jane, the parents received a letter from a man claiming to be in possession of the children. He said that he was willing to hand the children over to the parents at a specific time and location. The Beaumonts arrived at the appointed time and location with an undercover police officer but no one showed. They later received a letter from the same man claiming that he saw the undercover police officer arrive with the parents and that he would now keep the children, ending any hope of a peaceful exchange.

In 1992, following another investigation and remarkable achievements in fingerprint technology, authorities identified the author of the letters as a local man who was just a teenager at the time of the hoax. He reportedly wrote and mailed the letters as "a joke."

False Closure

Then, in November 2013, South Australian police received an anonymous tip claiming that the children were buried underneath a warehouse located in North Plympton. Although radar identified "one small anomaly, which can indicate movement or objects within the soil," no evidence was ever found.

The Suspects

Bevan Spencer von Einem

Bevan Spencer von Einem has long been considered the prime suspect in the disappearance of the Beaumont children. Einem was convicted of the July 1983 murder of fifteen-year-old Richard Kelvin, son of a popular news reporter, in 1984. Police have long suspected Einem of working with a series of accomplices and of having committed other abductions and murders.

In 1983, a police informant known as "Mr. B" told police that Einem claimed to have taken three children from a beach to perform medical "experiments," claiming that he performed "brilliant surgery" on the three children before accidentally killing one of them. Following the child's accidental death, the informant stated that Einem claimed to have killed the other two children and buried them in an open field outside the city of Adelaide.

Einem did bare some resemblance to the descriptions of the tall blond man given to police following the disappearance of the Beaumont children and was known to frequent Glenely Beach to spy on people in the changing rooms. He was also noted as having an obsession with children.

Einem worked as an accountant and lived with his mother. There were rumors that he was part of a ring of Adelaide professionals who shared a "hobby" of kidnapping, drugging and raping boys.

"Einem did match the description of the police sketches," Orange said. "And he did like to frequent the same beach. He seemed more interested in young teenage males as his list of known victims would indicate. Einem was a homosexual who picked up hitchhikers with his transvestite friend where they would engage in a "rough trade" style of sex. He would take photographs of his victims as a keepsake. The three young children would seem to be outside of his modus operandi."

However, Einem was significantly younger than the suspect described by witnesses; Einem was around 20 years old at the time, while the description of the suspect placed him in his late 20s. But, in 2007 local police officers identified a young man who looked exactly like a young Einem in Channel 7 news footage of the incident taken days after the disappearance. He remains a prime suspect in the case.

"The newly found news footage does implicate Einem in a psychological way," Orange said. "Killers often like to return to the scene of the crime. He was spotted on film, days after the disappearance. What are the odds against that?"

Arthur Stanley Brown

Arthur Stanley Brown, along with Einem, is considered to be one of two prime suspects in the abduction of the Beaumont children. In 1988, Brown, then 86 years old, was charged with kidnapping, raping, and murdering Judith and Susan Mackey in Townsville, Queensland. His first trial was declared a mistrial after the jury failed to reach a verdict in the case and his second trial was blocked because he was declared unfit to stand trial; Brown was suffering from dementia and Alzheimer's disease by this time.

He is considered one of two prime suspects in the case because of his connection to the murder of other children and because of his remarkable resemblance to descriptions of the tall blond man seen with the children at the time of their disappearance. He was also a prime suspect in the Adelaide Oval case, which involved the disappearance of Joanna Ratcliffe and Kirste Gordon.

"Brown was a known pedophile by his closest family members," Orange said. "He is alleged to have molested numerous younger relatives. He could be placed in the same area and time of the Beaumont children but nothing could be proven."

Although Brown is considered to be a prime suspect in the disappearance of the Beaumont children, the suspect in the case was identified as being in his late 30s; Brown was in his 50s at the time. Brown died in 2002 without ever admitting to the crime.

"Brown would move into a nursing home at the end of his life," Orange said. "He would die an innocent man with the courts never able to officially charge him because of his Alzheimer's."

James Ryan O'Neill

James Ryan O'Neill, convicted of murdering nine-year-old Ricky John Smith in the Australian state of Tasmania in 1975 and currently serving a life sentence for the crime, was considered as a suspect in the Beaumont children disappearance for some time. He is reported as having told several friends in the early 1970s that he was responsible for the disappearance of the Beaumont children in 1966. However, he was publicly eliminated as a suspect by the South Australian police. He remains in prison in Tasmania to this day.

"O'Neill was the subject of a documentary called 'The Fishermen,'" Orange said. "In the documentary, he is evasive about being the man behind the disappearance of the children. He is, however, at the forefront of most pundits who have studied the story. While Brown and Einem did not have charming personas, O'Neill did. He was handsome and smiley with the ability to manipulate everyone around him. He could fabricate lies at the drop of a hat so it is easy to believe that he would be able to charm the children into his acquaintance. People who knew him all described him as 'the most likable man you'll ever meet.' No one could believe that he would be capable of such an act."

Derek Ernest Percy

In 2007, the Victorian newspaper The Age published a report stating that Derek Ernest Percy, at the time the longest-serving prisoner in the southeastern Australian state, was responsible for the disappearance of the Beaumont children in 1966. Initially jailed in 1970 for the 1969 murder of 12-year-old Yvonne Tuohy, Percy was found not guilty of the crime by reason of insanity, but was nonetheless jailed "indefinitely."

He is widely considered to be Australia's worst child serial killer and is suspected of the killings of the Beaumont children, as well as the abduction, attempted rape, and stabbing of Marianne Schmidt and Christine Sharrock on January 11, 1965. In October 2014, Percy was also ruled to have abducted and killed seven-year-old Linda Stilwell in

1968. However, Percy passed away from cancer in 2013, having never admitted to any of his crimes. He remains a possible suspect in the case.

"Percy is unique in that he may have had his mother not aiding him but covering up for him," Orange said. "He is certainly one of the most sadistic pedophiles on record, his doings are unmentionable out of respect for his victims. He was in the city at the time of the Beaumont children disappearance and is probably the top suspect along with O'Neill. His mother, however, has thrown out a lot of what could have been evidence in the case."

Related Cases

Two similar cases to the disappearance of the Beaumont children attracted widespread attention in the South Australian media, and the primary suspect in the Beaumont children's kidnapping case was convicted in one case and suspected in the other.

The Adelaide Oval Case

On August 25, 1972, two young girls, Joanne Ratcliffe (aged 11) and Kirste Gordon (aged 4) went missing while attending an Australian football game. They are presumed dead. This case also received widespread attention in the South Australian media and Bevan Spencer von Einem was considered the primary suspect in their disappearance.

Einem matched the descriptions of the tall blond man provided by witnesses in the Beaumont children's case and closely resembles the police sketch released to the public. A private police report in leaked in 1989 identified Einem as the primary suspect in the case.

The Family Murders

From 1973 to 1983, a group of men is believed to have been involved in the abduction, rape, and murder of a series of young men and male teenagers in the Adelaide area. Five teens were killed during this time period, including Alan Barnes (aged 16), Neil Muir (aged 25), Peter Stogneff (aged 14), Mark Langley (aged 18), and Richard Kelvin (aged 15). All victims were abducted and subjected to extended bouts of torture and physical assault, including sexual assault and medical experimentation.

Bevan Spencer von Einem was convicted of the abduction and murder of Richard Kelvin 1984 and is currently serving life in prison in Port Augusta prison. In 1990, he was also charged with the murder of Alan Barnes and Mark Langley, but key evidence from the Richard Kelvin murder was ruled inadmissible in the trial. Following the ruling against this key evidence, the prosecution dropped these charges against Einem on December 21, 1990.

Although Einem was the only member of this group to be convicted, and four out of five of The Family Murders remain unsolved, law enforcement officials believe that Einem was part of a white-collar group that preyed on young children. He remains the prime, and only living, suspect in the disappearance of the Beaumont children.

Impact on the Parents

Jim and Nancy Beaumont continued to hold out hope of finding their children for several decades after their disappearance. In fact, the couple continued to live at the Somerton Park home, at 109 Harding Street, that they shared with their children for nearly two decades, hoping that the children would return home someday. Nancy Beaumont was reported as saying that it would be "dreadful" if the children returned to the home only to find that their parents had moved.

"The Beaumonts left the rooms of the children untouched," Orange said. "Every toy, every book even the bed was left exactly as the children had left them."

The couple were never considered as suspects in the case and cooperated with the police at every turn in the investigation, including working with the police and searching in vain every time a new lead developed in the case over the next several decades.

According to The Age, the parents "have since separated, but still live in Adelaide." The stress and sorrow that resulted from their children's abduction, combined with the constant new leads and media attention is said to have contributed to the failure of their marriage.

Jim, in particular, is said to still be suffering from intense and inconsolable grief every time a new development is reported. Nancy was also reported to have suffered extreme grief and horror when, in 1990, several Australian newspapers released computer-generated images of what her children would look like after aging several decades. She reportedly refused to look at the pictures.

"Jim was a little bit stronger than Nancy," Orange said. "He would address the media more than she did. But they both suffered terribly for the rest of their lives into their eighties. They would spend over fifty years wishing for their children's return, getting false hope after false hope, one false lead after another which would all ultimately turn up nothing. It was a horrific cruelty."

Lastly, Jim and Nancy have largely been seen as sympathetic and pitiable figures in the Australian media and in society at large. Although their actions may seem reckless or irresponsible by today's standards, Australian society was viewed as extremely safe in the 1960s and their policy of allowing a child to supervise their younger siblings both in the home and in public was practiced by a large portion of Australian parents.

Impact on Australian Society

The disappearance of the Beaumont children became an overnight sensation in Australia, led to one of the largest police searches in the country's history, and remains the most famous missing persons case in the country. Prior to this incident, Australia was largely viewed as one of the safest societies on the planet and children were allowed to roam freely, doors remained unlocked at all times, and there was little fear of strangers. All of that changed overnight.

"Australia lost its innocence with the disappearance of the Beaumont Children," Orange said. "For three young children to disappear was unheard of. The city where they grew up was a dignified place, a safe place. But it was all an illusion that went away the day the children went missing."

During the initial search for the children, Jim Beaumont went on national television to appeal for their safe return. His heartfelt address to the nation had a lasting impact on the parents and children who watched his plea. Hundreds of viewers called into the station to offer tips and Australian police report that hundreds of tips continue to come in every year to this day. His image on national television continues to serve as a warning for those who believe in the incorruptibility of their fellow citizens and in the safety of their country.

"A lot of people today will blame the parents for letting them go on the bus alone," Adelaide resident Rachel Harding said. "But times were different back then. Back then kids would walk to school by themselves. Kids were told not to talk to strangers. The Beaumonts did tell their children to not talk to children. But child molesters are cunning monsters. My guess is that he may have stolen the eldest child's purse then conned them into seeing him as their benefactor. They would not have had money to get home then along comes this "blonde man" who offers them money. Buys them food and promises to take them home."

Children who came of age in Australia during the 1960s have remarked that there was a definite culture shift following the Beaumont children's disappearance, often describing a "before" and "after." While children were once allowed to roam freely and interact with strangers, Australian parents have since altered their style of parenting and curtailed the amount of freedom offered to young children.

"It was the type of case where we believe there was a lone offender," Australian police detective Des Bray said. "It isn't the type of crime where one would go around bragging about. But we do hope that he told someone and that somebody knows something."

If the Beaumont children are alive today, they would all be in their 50s and would have lived through years of hearing their names and story broadcast on national television and reported on breathlessly in national newspapers. Despite the vast amount of information we have on the case, their fates may never be known with any certainty.

Both Jim and Nancy Beaumont are still alive, and as of this writing they are ninety and eighty-years old respectively. The anonymous tips and false hopes continue to come in today as they did over fifty years ago.

THE MISSING BEAUTY QUEEN : THE DISAPPEARANCE OF TARA GRINSTEAD

AMANDA DARLING

"I'm an 11th-grade history teacher at Irwin County High school. I also have a cheerleading squad of Junior Varsity cheerleaders. I just completed my first year of teaching, and I love every bit of it." - Tara Grinstead in a 1999 interview.

Tara Grinstead was a beauty pageant winner and high school teacher who strangely disappeared on October 22nd, 2005.

The mystery of her disappearance is as baffling now as it was over ten years ago. Tara was a beautiful woman in a small town and drew the attention of many men. But as investigators peeled back the onion on her life, they discovered that she had a complex personal life, one with many lovers and layers of relationship any one of whom may have sought to do her harm out of jealousy.

Investigators have pieced together the timeline of her activities prior to her disappearance. But the missing piece lies sometime during the night of October 22nd, 2005, when someone abducted Tara Grinstead and she would never be seen again.

What happened to Tara Grinstead?

EARLY LIFE

Tara was born on November 14th, 1974 to Faye and Billy Grinstead. She grew up in Hawkinsville, Georgia and was a popular cheerleader in high school as well as a diligent student. Her parents would divorce and her father would remarry a woman named Connie to whom Tara grew close to as well.

Tara loved animals, singing and going to church as a kid.

One cannot look upon pictures and video of Tara and not remark that she had a striking beauty. Graced with a voluptuous figure and long black hair, she had the ability to light up any room she walked into. She would eventually compete in beauty pageants, falling in love with the preparation, competition, and glamor of the activity.

"She had been into so many (pageants) that I had lost count," Connie Grinstead said.

Tara meticulously prepared for the pageants, remaining physically fit, taking speech lessons and learning how to sing. She would also graduate from Middle Georgia College and become a teacher at Irwin County High School in Ocilla. She would teach history to 11th graders but not give up on her pageant hopes.

In 1999, she would achieve the first step in her dream to enter the Miss USA contest, when she would win the local title of Miss Tifton.

This victory would allow her to compete in the Miss Georgia pageant. She would also receive scholarship winnings that she would use to help pay for her continuing college education.

"It was, for her, more than a dream come true," Tara's best friend Maria Hulett said. "It was the chance for her to be really proud of herself."

Footage of Tara during the Georgia pageant showed her to be an exuberant woman with a zest for life. She loved to exercise, drink Diet Coke with grenadine, collect Barbies and listening to 80s music like Bon Jovi. She had an infectious smile and played to the camera as she showed off her yellow business suit that she would wear for the pageant interview.

"Why did you pick yellow?" the reporter asked.

"Because it shows that I'm a happy person," Tara said.

With her pageant days behind her, Tara would earn a master's degree in education from Valdosta State University.

"She wanted to be a principal," her friend Oshja Anderson said. "She was well on her way."

Always seeking to improve herself, Tara would teach classes during the day and go to graduate school at night. She also held down a part-time job selling cosmetics at the local department store. By 2005, she had applied for a doctoral program in history and would occasionally fill in as the assistant principal.

"On the surface," forensic psychiatrist Orange said. "Tara's life looked to be a stellar one. She had a bright future in academia and during her pageant days, she learned to put forward the best appearance. But what lurked underneath in her personal life is the mystery."

MARCUS HARPER

At the heart of Tara's disappearance is figuring out the type of relationships she had with the numerous men in her life. She worked as a teacher, went to night school and worked the cosmetics counter at a department store. Outgoing and bubbly, she didn't have the personality type to reject anyone out of hand. She attracted men and had many suitors.

She did have a longtime boyfriend in Marcus Harper.

Harper was an Ocilla police officer who would later become an Army Ranger. Both of Tara's parents liked him as they both expressed the fact that he always remained respectful of them. They have consistently maintained that they never witnessed Harper treating Tara with disrespect.

Tara, however, had expressed to her sister that she was afraid of Marcus.

"She said she was afraid of him," Tara's sister Anita said. "What he had gone through with the Ranger training. He was capable of anything."

"Marcus was a strong Alpha-male type," Orange said. "A cop and an Army Ranger. Tara was rumored to have dated another cop as well but she didn't appear to have a type. From what we can gather, she dated a slew of men from older to younger, and from different walks of life."

About a year prior to her disappearance, Tara had broken up with Marcus. She had given him an ultimatum and wanted to be married. He did not want marriage but wanted to remain committed. The relationship would turn sour at that point.

Tara would begin to date other people. She was in a car with a romantic suitor named Rhett Roberts who was the son of her landlord. Marcus spotted the couple and would go ballistic, shouting obscenities at Tara.

Despite this angry confrontation, Tara would maintain ties with Marcus. In late July or early August of 2005 they would go to St. Augustine on a beach trip. After their date, Tara would confide to a friend that she was concerned about Marcus's temper.

Marcus would then be deployed back to Iraq a few weeks later. Tara would write the Army Ranger a letter in which she effectively ended their relationship.

According to Marcus, however, their relationship didn't come to a close until October of 2005. He had returned from the Middle East and called Tara to tell her that their relationship was over. Tara was at work and became so distraught that had to pull over to the side of the road. She called a friend who came and took her home. The next day, Tara would call off sick from her teaching job in order to "take a mental health day."

There was a rumor that a cop from a neighboring town, Heath Dykes, came to visit Tara at her school shortly afterward.

"These behaviors certainly show some mental fragilities on the parts of both Tara and Marcus," Orange said. "From what we can gather, it looked like an off-and-on style relationship with a few other romantic partners thrown in for good measure. It is unclear as to who was chasing who at various points of their relationship. If we are to believe Marcus, then she was chasing him. If we are to believe Tara's sister, then she was afraid of him. Why would you chase a man that you were afraid of? Something is not right here."

A few days later, Tara and Marcus would have another "heated argument" which she would tell one of her friends at her night class as well as another friend the next day while she had lunch.

According to Marcus, the argument centered around him breaking up with her. But Tara's sister Anita Gattis had a different story.

"They had a very bad argument," Anita said. "Several days before she went missing, concerning an 18-year-old that he was dating. My sister did not think that (the 18-year-old's) parents would approve of a

30-year-old dating an-18-year-old. I'm told that she threatened to tell the parents and they had a very heated argument over this."

Marcus said the argument was about something else entirely. He stated that she begged him not to end their relationship.

"She wanted me back and all," Marcus said. "And I said, 'I've started shopping outside of Ocilla, I think you need to do the same. Everybody in this town is connected to us one way or another."

"She approached me crying," Harper said as he repeated the same story on Greta Van Susteren's TV show. "She was very irrational, and she told me that if she found out I was dating someone, she would commit suicide."

But Tara's friend Osjha disputes the fact that Tara would do or say something like that.

"She's never said anything remotely similar to me ever any time."

Law enforcement authorities don't believe Tara committed suicide as she would have to go to extreme lengths to hide her own body and would have no motive to do so.

"There are a couple of contradictory things at play here," Orange said. "Tara was rumored to have dated some of her students so it would be hypocritical of her to criticize Marcus for dating someone in their teens. And it also doesn't make sense for her to come to Marcus' home begging to get back together. She had her share of suitors, some coming from out of town. She was a beautiful woman and she had options."

To her family's dismay, both the authorities and press would place Tara's life under a microscope. They had discovered that she had "several romantic relationships that occurred in relative proximity to one another."

"There was more rumors and innuendo," Orange said. "There were rumors that she was dating Rhett Roberts, her landlord's son. Rumors that she was dating one of her teenage students. Rumors that she was dating Heath Dyke, a police officer from another county. Even her own brother-in-law, Larry Gattis, was rumored to have an affair with Tara."

Both Larry and Tara's sisters are physicians. Larry specializes in geriatric medicine with only 3.3 out of 5-star reviews on Healthgrades. He was interrogated by investigators and expressed his outrage at the questions they were asking. One question was that if he had an affair with Tara and his response was judged by the polygraph as "deceptive."

ALL THAT AND A STALKER TOO...

Tara would have a stalker in a former student named Anthony Vickers. Friends recalled that Tara had taken special care to tutor Vickers but she later realized that the young man was "unstable."

"He was just kind of a troubled kid and that would be her nature," Osjha said.

Vickers was obsessed with his beauty queen teacher and claimed to have had a romantic relationship with her.

"She talked about the fact that he would call and he would rely on her and she knew it was getting too much for her," a friend named Maria said. "I just kept telling her, 'You know Tara, something's wrong.'"

Vickers was two years out of high school when he came to Tara's house and demanded to be let in. He pounded on the door until she called the police. Vickers resisted arrest but charges were later dropped and no restraining orders were ever filed.

The Vickers incident wasn't the only occasion that the former beauty pageant winner was being stalked. There was an incident where someone would call her home and make threats. The call was traced and it was determined to be a student in her homeroom who was promptly removed from the class.

THE NIGHT OF...

Before the night of her disappearance, Tara had enjoyed the company of her friend Dana and some teenage girls as they readied for the "Miss Georgia Sweet Potato" pageant. Her friend remembered Tara as being in a great mood, helping out the girls with their hair and makeup. She would attend the pageant where she served as a backstage coach. Later that evening, she went to the house of a neighbor before going to a barbecue a few blocks from her home . Police believe that she had remained at the barbecue until 11 pm when she left to go home. They would find the clothes she wore at the cookout on her bedroom floor which indicated to police that she had, in fact, returned home.

From that point on, police "have no idea" what happened to Tara.

On October 24th, 2005, Tara did not show up to teach her class. Her colleagues called the police who showed up at her residence to do a welfare check. They would find her white Mitsubishi parked in the garage, unlocked. Upon entering her home, police found a business card lodged in her door.

There appeared to be no sign of forced entry. Searching through the house, police found her cell phone plugged into her charger. Her purse and keys could not be found.

Strangely, the clothes she wore the night before were piled on the bedroom floor.

Investigators found it odd that the car door was unlocked and that the car seat was pushed back. Tara was petite at only five-foot-three and would have kept the seat much closer to the steering wheel. They found an envelope of cash (one hundred dollars) on her dashboard while both her dog and cat were inside. Tara's sister said that she was an animal lover who would never just abandon her pets.

Something was wrong...

The police immediately called the Georgia Bureau of Investigation as the lacked the resources to pursue this kind of crime.

Taking over the case, the GBI believed that Tara may have left with someone that she knew, given the lack of a forced entry and the fact that only her purse and keys were missing. Neighbors did not report hearing any screaming at night.

Her disappearance shocked the small and close-knit community. To a person, Tara was described as someone who had a great personality, loved by faculty and students alike. Nothing in her professional life would suggest that she had any enemies.

Volunteers from the community immediately went to work. Irwin County students, teachers, and other townsfolk searched the area and put out flyers.

"Missing. Tara Grinstead. $20,000 Reward."

ROUNDING UP THE SUSPECTS

Longtime boyfriend Marcus Harper was one of the first to be questioned. He came with a ready-made alibi for the night of Tara's disappearance.

Marcus was seen at a bar with friends then went on a 'ride-along' with a former partner on the local police force. His whereabouts was "essentially substantiated" according to authorities.

Former student/stalker Anthony Vickers was questioned but later ruled out as a suspect. Like the others, however, he could not account for the entire thirty-four hour period when Tara was last seen and reported missing.

"Vickers is probably the only one I would rule out," Orange said. "This disappearance was too clean. Vickers was a disturbed twenty-year-old man with a crush. He would not have the emotional wherewithal or the knowledge to pull off a crime with no clues. But someone with law enforcement or medical training could."

But who left the business card behind at her door?

The card was left by Heath Dykes, a married Perry police officer with two children. He was from the next town over and had known Tara since high school.

Neighbors would tell investigators that he visited Tara's house often. It is unclear what their relationship was (outside of the obvious innuendo and rumors).

Still, he had left close to two dozen messages on Tara's answering message on the weekend she went missing.

There is small-town gossip that the two were having an affair. Local witnesses have confirmed that they saw his wife throw his clothes out on the front lawn. The content of the messages he left have not been made public but the rumors were that he was telling her "he was sorry" and that he "loved her."

What is clear is that he did call Tara's mother from the front yard and ask if she knew where Tara was and if she was alright.

Heath Dykes was the last known person at Tara's home that night as he arrived a little after midnight.

"There are simply too many secrets here," Orange said. "Something was clearly going on in Heath's mind in order for him to call Tara that many times over the course of one evening. One rumor is that they were having an affair and that she was going to tell his wife. So he was calling her in a desperate attempt to stop her from doing that. Another possibility was that she was calling him for help and he was returning her calls. His involvement led to a lot of outlandish speculation, one of which was that Heath knew that a hit man was coming for Tara and that he was calling to make sure that she was okay."

"I think the fact that she was beautiful and other people paid attention to her would obviously make some people jealous," Tara's friend Maria said. "I think she was afraid of the possibility of someone hurting her from being angry at her, having reactions to her dating people."

Numerous men were rounded up and questioned, there was Jim Perry who dated Tara years earlier, Rhett Roberts, Marcus Harper, Anthony Vickers, and Eric Cook among others.

Another unsubstantiated rumor that Tara was involved with another student named Eric Cook. A friend of his had made mention of their affair in an Internet forum post where he stated that everyone knew that they were "messing around." He also said that the police didn't make the information public out of respect for Tara's family as she dated around quite a bit. An alleged friend of Cook disputed the rumor on the forum, however. Cook would later die in a car accident.

A neighbor, Joe Poirier lived with his wife and was rumored to have been "obsessed" with Tara. The older couple admitted to "looking out for

Tara" and they were fond of her. He was seen pouring concrete near his home the day after she disappeared.

Another person of interest was Larry Gattis, the brother-in-law of Tara. He was brought in for questioning after the disappearance. It would later be revealed that he had been asked if he had an affair with Tara.

Larry answered 'no.'

The polygraph machine marked it as a 'deceptive answer.'

48 HOURS

In 2008, Tara's case would be featured on the CBS News show "48 Hours Mystery." The show would illustrate the parallels between Tara's case and the disappearance of Jennifer Kesse who would go missing in Orlando, Florida three months later. The GBI would also reveal during the broadcast that they had found a latex glove in Tara's yard just a few feet away from her front porch.

The GBI forensic team would analyze the DNA left in the glove and determine that it was a man's DNA, they just do not know who it belongs to. They would compare the DNA samples of the numerous men who were associated with or knew Tara but none of them have matched.

The DNA has also been entered into the Georgia and national databases but no match has been made to date.

"The glove may be a red herring," Orange said. "Whoever entered the home left nothing behind, no prints, DNA, nothing. So it was obviously someone who knew exactly what they were doing. They wanted to harm Tara."

A HOAX AND FALSE TIPS

In February of 2009, a man calling himself the "Catch Me Killer" began posting videos boasting that he had murdered sixteen women. One of the women he described had a close resemblance to Tara Grinstead. The man producing the video digitally obscured his face and voice but police eventually identified the culprit as twenty-seven-year-old Andrew Haley.

Haley performed the videos as part of a bizarre hoax and was eliminated as a possible suspect.

Investigator Gary Rothwell has expressed his lament at how the rumors and speculation have caused unfair stress to many who have been already tried in the public eye. "Irresponsible public accusations have been made about them, and they have no way to respond or defend themselves. And it's frustrating that we don't have evidence to rule anyone in or out."

Rothwell admits, however, that he has information that has not been released.

In February of 2015, authorities acted on a tip which led them to drain a pond in Fitzgerald, Georgia.

They didn't go into details as to what the specifics of the tip were. The pond would be drained and nothing would be found.

ALIBIS

Police have alibis from all the men who knew Tara Grinstead but no one has been ruled out because no one can account for the full thirty-four hour period.

Rhett Reynolds stated he went to sleep after the cookout. Joe Poirier was with his wife next door.

The most elaborate alibi, however, came from Marcus Harper.

Again, Marcus was in a local bar and a friend of Tara's had spotted him there. She would call Tara at around 10:15 and 10:30 to tell Tara that Marcus was there.

After 1 am, Marcus left the bar and went to look for his police officer friend, Sgt. Sean Fletcher. Fletcher was on duty that night.

Fletcher knew Tara as well. Ironically, he was one of the officers who arrived at Tara's house when Anthony Vickers, Tara's former student, was banging on her door.

There were rumors that Tara didn't like Fletcher because he had told Harper that Tara was entertaining Heath Dykes at her home.

Fletcher would deny that speculation.

"What we can extrapolate from this scenario was that Vickers was angry that his crush, Tara, was with another man," Orange said. "So he goes to her home and demands that she talk to him. He's young, twenty-years-old, and doesn't understand why she would do this to him. He is then arrested by Fletcher who relays what Tara is doing to Marcus, a man that Tara is wary about because of his temper. So now we have more than just a love triangle, it is a love octagon, with numerous men vying for and getting jealous over the attention of Tara."

At around 1:49 am, Fletcher received a call from dispatch informing him that Marcus Harper was looking for him. The two met up and walked Fletcher's beat, checking doors in downtown Ocilla.

Around 2:45, Fletcher was dispatch to a home where a mentally unbalanced man, Bennie Merritt, had stumbled into a home and refused to leave. Marcus would join Fletcher on the call as did two other officers. Merritt, however, was gone from the premises.

Minutes later, they began to search for Merritt who was also a neighbor of Tara's. The drunken Merritt would accost the cashier at the local gas station then be apprehended. Both Fletcher and Harper had responded to the call at the gas station and by the time they were done it was 4:28 am.

Marcus then headed home.

Investigators would later be able to corroborate these details with multiple witnesses, including Merritt, who was scrutinized as a possible suspect in the kidnapping as well.

Marcus Harper, however, has not been ruled out as a potential person of interest in the case.

"Marcus's alibi is too perfect," GBI investigator Maurice Godwin said.

Both Larry and Anita Gattis believe that Marcus is the top suspect.

"He had the motive," Tara's sister said. "And the training."

The insinuation would draw the ire of Marcus who became upset that Anita consistently brought up his military and police training. He continues to deny any involvement in Tara's disappearance.

"I don't wanna hurt any innocent civilian much less someone I spent five and a half years of my life with."

"What is clear is that there isn't a whole lot forthcoming about Tara's personal life to draw the conclusions we need to about who is the most probable suspect," Orange said. "Like in the Natalee Holloway case, the sexual activity of the woman in question is kept hidden. If her background reveals that she was a promiscuous woman, there will e less sympathy and urgency to solve the crime. That is one of the more striking aspects of the case, aside from Tara's vanishing, is the cover-up of Tara's personal life in order to protect her reputation."

UNSOLVABLE CASE?

Tara Grinstead's case is still being investigated. The GBI reports that they receive numerous leads per day, most of which are false.

Her body has never been found but her impact on the lives of those around her and her students will never be forgotten.

"I'm so sorry to hear about what happened to Miss Grinstead," said Christine Kang, a South Korean exchange student from Grinstead's class. "She is so caring and giving to her students. I am sure she will come home soon safely. I will pray for her every night."

MISTY COPSEY

Misty Copsey was fourteen years old when she disappeared on September 17th, 1992 after a trip to the Puyallup Fair.

Her case remains a showcase of administrative screw-ups and dropped balls. She was initially thought of as a runaway before foul play was finally suspected a month after the fact. Subsequently, there have been at least five people suspected of committing her abduction.

But the Puyallup police did not get within sniffing distance of Misty or charging anyone with her disappearance. Three different police chiefs and numerous detectives all took a swing at the case and whiffed. No one in law enforcement has been able to answer the question on everyone's lips.

What happened to Misty Copsey?

A GOOD GIRL

Misty was born in 1978 to Diana and Paul "Buck" Copsey. Her father was a firefighter but the couple split up shortly after she was born and Misty lived with her mother.

Misty got good grades in school, excelling particularly in Math. During her last quarter at Spanaway Lake Junior High School, she got A's and B's. Athletic, she played softball, volleyball, and basketball before breaking both forearms during an athletic practice.

Misty was not the ringleader of a bad crowd. She was diffident but funny, entertaining her friends while skipping around and singing the theme song to Sesame Street.

She did not have much in regards to material wants. Her mother eked out a living as an in-home care nurse and they lived in a mobile home park until she was fourteen. Seeking a better place to live, Diana and Misty moved into a duplex where she now had her own room. But Misty longed for her friend who lived in and around the old trailer park. She would make it back there when she could to just hang out.

Tall, blonde and with green eyes, Misty was cute enough to draw the attention of boys. She remained chaste, however, and was not dating like so many of her other friends.

Her innocent, girl-next-door looks would draw the attention of Rheuban Schmidt. Rheuban looked like a casting call actor for a meth head. He sported a reverse mullet, a hairstyle that was cut close to the sides with curls on top. He had beady, green eyes that screamed low IQ. One of Misty's friends described him as a "scuzzy looking dude" but he nonetheless befriends Misty, much to the chagrin of her mother.

Diana grew suspicious of the relationship as Rheuban was four years older and a high school dropout. On one occasion, she listened in on the other end of a phone conversation Misty was having with Rheuban.

"I get horny just looking at you, Misty," Rheuban said, whispering like an old pervert.

Diana became enraged and ordered her daughter off the phone.

"Don't ever talk to that idiot again...."

ENTER CORY BOBER

Cory Bober was a thorn in the side of police every since the Green River killings became a national news story. He would insist that the police are "incompetent fools" while organizing his own searches for her remains. Diana would later accuse him of killing her daughter but he would respond by telling Diana that she was being "ungrateful." He was, after all, the only man on the case.

Bober was a recluse without a vehicle or a drive's license. An inveterate marijuana user, he had a record for both possession and dealing. He was also obsessed with cases of murdered or slain women in his home state of Washington. He had a stack of binders with autopsy reports, pictures, and other arcane details.

Bober came under the radar of the police in Puyallup when he became obsessed with the Green River Killer case. He had a brief acquaintance with Randall Dean Achziger, remembering a conversation where the man told him that the killer inserted rocks into the remains of his victim. Bober became suspicious as that would turn out to be a piece of information only known to police. He then went on a one-man crusade to prove the guilt of Achziger. Bober would interview his ex-girlfriends, friends, co-workers and present all of this in an affidavit to the courts.

Achziger found it ridiculous and annoying.

So did the police.

The Green River Killer would turn out to be a painter named Gary Leon Ridgway.

Bober didn't give up, however. He knew Achziger was the guy.

Bober had his own theories about who was performing the killings. Some were wild and outlandish conspiracy theories. Others were spot on. He would notice that there were victims that "had disappeared on the very same date that others were discovered. Some victims seemed to almost 'commemorate' the deaths or discoveries of others; one would die on a particular date and another would disappear a year to the day later on the very same date."

The police dismissed his theories as the rantings of a crack head. But Bober would be willing to show the proof of his connect the dots calculations. He pointed to the cases of Kim Delange, a 15-year-old killed in 1988 and Anna Chebetnoy, a 14-year-old killed in 1990. Both of their bodies would be found along Highway 410, east of Enumclaw.

Bober discovered that the remains of both girls were found in the same section of 410. The girls were found two years and one month apart. He felt that the killer was following a pattern.

He called the police department and left a voice mail. He predicted that a teen girl from Puyallup would disappear and her remains would be found on Highway 410 in the same vicinity where the other girl's bodies were found. Bober gave him the name of the man whom he felt was the serial killer.

Randall Achziger.

But the police were now used to his calls and viewed him as a crank. A nutcake with a strange vendetta.

His prediction would be half-right, however.

There would be no body found on Highway 410.

But a teenage girl would disappear.

Her name was Misty Copsey.

A NIGHT AT THE FAIR

On September 17th, 1992, Diana told her daughter Misty and her best friend Trina Bevard to behave themselves. Misty had convinced her mother to let them stay out that night…free of any meddlesome adults. But Trina's guardian would not allow her to go without an adult driving them home.

Diana worked as a caregiver for a 97-year-old Alzheimer patient who could not be left alone. She would not be able to drive the girls home. But Misty checked the bus schedules and convinced her mother that they would be okay. There was a bus that left the fair at 8:40 p.m.

Misty then convinced her mother to lie to Trina's guardian, Marlene Shoemaker.

"No worries," Diana said to Marlene. "I'll bring them home."

She wanted to be the cool parent, different from the stuffy adults who forgot what it was like to be fourteen. If it meant telling a white lie so her little girl could have some happiness, so be it.

What was the worst that could happen?

Diana dropped the girls off and gave them one last warning.

"Get home safe."

It would be the last time she would ever see her daughter again.

THE PHONE CALL

A few hours later, Diana would then receive a phone call from Misty as she tended to her elderly patient. Misty told her that she had missed the bus but could get a ride from Rheuban Schmidt.

Diana, knowing what kind of unsavory character Schmidt was, adamantly refused. She told Misty to find someone else to give her a ride back. Misty had an electronic diary which she used to store phone numbers. She told her mother she would find someone trustworthy to call for a ride.

"You call me back when you find someone," Diana said.

"I will. I promise."

Diana would wait all night for the phone call.

In the ensuing hours, Misty would not call back.

Worried, Diane called home in the hope that Misty had gotten a ride without calling her.

No answer.

Diana didn't panic. She figured that Misty went home with that scumbag Schmidt and didn't want to get yelled out for disobeying her.

She's going to get yelled at either/or. All Diana wanted was for her daughter to be safe.

Her shift finally ended and Diana drove back home in a rush.

Upon entering her house, she called out for Misty.

Silence.

She went into Misty's room and saw that it had been untouched from the previous night.

Diana would call the police in a panic. She told them that her daughter had not come home from the fair. The dispatcher would tell her that the police could not do anything about it for thirty days as it "sounded like a runaway case."

Diana knew otherwise.

Trying to calm herself, she figured that Misty was with Trina, that the two of them would be okay.

She called Trina's home.

No answer.

She then began scorching the earth with phone calls.

She would call Rheuban but he told her that she called but he didn't have the gas to go get her. She then called numerous friends of Misty and her mother.

No one had seen Misty.

She called Trina's home again, got no answer, then drove out to her house. She then went to the police department and filed a formal report with the Pierce County's Sheriff's Department who handled runaways as opposed to the Puyallup Police.

MISTY'S MISSING

Misty's friend Trina called Diana after she came back from school. She told the frantic mother that she didn't know where Misty was.

"The last time I saw her, she was heading for the bus," she said.

Diana would call Rheuban again. She would get his roommate this time, James Tinsley.

Diana needed answers. She interrogated the young fifteen-year-old like a grizzled police detective. She asked if Rheuban had been home all night. James then told her that Rheuban and his uncle went to pick up Misty but that he wasn't home just yet.

Later, Diana would call back and Rheuban would tell her that his roommate got the story wrong. He went to a party instead and didn't pick up Misty. He didn't know where she was.

Diana pleaded for the police to do something. They dragged their heels and began talking to some of Misty's friends. "Just call if she calls," they informed them. "No one gets in trouble."

Diana printed fliers with Misty's picture. She plastered them in and around the fairgrounds while calling the media.

The one woman search team would yield no leads. Rheuban would stop by and ask if the police had found anything yet. Diana would then wait at the bus stop near the fairgrounds to inquire with different drivers on the route. She found one driver who said that he saw Misty. She had asked when the next bus to Spanaway was arriving. The driver said it wasn't and that he was done for the night. He gave her instructions on which bus to take but she walked away before he could complete his sentence.

AN ERROR OF JUDGEMENT

Among the many mistakes that the Puyallup police made in the investigation of Misty's disappearance was to make the assumption that she was a runaway. Why they didn't entertain the prospect that she could have been kidnapped and murdered gave the abductor precious time to cover his tracks.

The police came to this erroneous conclusion after they interviewed Misty's mother, Diana. They thought she was a liar and an alcoholic. They then interviewed a pair of Misty's classmates who really didn't know her that well or accompany her to the fair.

A series of cover-ups then ensued, as the police told the media Misty had been found (where they got that information remains a mystery) and made no further investigation.

Until Diana and the media started to make a fuss. The department had to save face and eventually one of the detectives believed that this was not a runaway case.

Misty's disappearance could not be ignored any longer.

Police would talk to the various fair workers and security guards. No one had recalled seeing Misty.

The police then turned to her family, interviewing and doing background checks on both Misty's father, Buck, and Diana.

Their impressions of the duo would support their initial theory that Misty runaway. Diana was an alcoholic with multiple DUIs and seven years prior she had been convicted of welfare fraud. Buck confirmed that his daughter and Diana would have their issues.

Carver then discovered that Diana had filed a runaway report on Misty a month prior to her disappearing.

Diana would later state that the report was wrong. She thought Misty had disappeared then found her in the bedroom. She was too ashamed to tell the police it had been a false alarm.

With the police questioning and media coverage, Misty Copsey was now the talk of her Spanaway Lake Junior High school.

Rumors would abound at the school, one of which came from Misty Matthews who said that Misty had called her from Olympia. Another student stated that she saw Misty at a Color Me Badd concert at the fair.

The rumors were enough to prompt Carver to remove Misty from the FBI's National Crime Information Center as a missing person. He would once again treat her as a runaway.

BOBER'S THEORY

Cory Bober's knew he was right. He knew that police would find a body of a young woman off Highway 410.

He waited but nothing happened.

Until his mother showed him the flier of Misty's disappearance.

Right again!

Heart racing, he called the number on the flier. Bober would get into contact with Diana and hurriedly told her all about his research.

He talked about the Green River Killer, where and how he killed his victims. He would tell Diana that her disappearance was connected to the same guy responsible for the murdered Puyallup Girls, Kim Delange and Anne Chebetnoy.

Cory would apologize to Diana because he knew that Misty was dead. He predicted her body would be found somewhere along Highway 410.

The two would form an uneasy alliance. Bober became Misty's personal avenger. He would start a phone/letter/media campaign to prove the police wrong and himself right.

Misty was no runaway.

She was a victim of Randall Achziger.

In October, however, Bober would be arrested for selling marijuana. He was then accosted by Sgt. Herm Carver who tired of the young man meddling in police affairs.

"He walked in the room I was being held in – looking tired and pissed off. He said, 'I got out of bed tonight, and came down here to meet you – just to see what kind of a hypocrite you REALLY ARE!'

I said (being cocky), 'It's not MY FAULT – HERM – that you don't believe Misty Copsey's MISSING!!'

He yelled (angry), 'DON'T YOU EVER CALL ME BY MY FIRST NAME – IT'S SGT. CARVER TO YOU!!!'"

Bober's journals, November 1992

THIRTY DAYS MISSING

Sgt. Herm Carver and Deputy Brian Coburn would each individually warn Diana of the troublemaker that Bober was. Still, the worried mother would welcome his assistance as she needed all the help she could get. After numerous phone calls, the two would finally meet after a month of Misty being missing. Diana had nowhere else to turn but to the shaggy-haired twenty-six-year-old who lived with his parents.

The police were going through the motions on their end. Carver reactivated Misty's name on state and national lists but only because he was legally required to do so. At this point, he still believed Misty to be a runaway and doubted Diana's veracity.

Meanwhile, Diana would find Cory Bober's constant badgering to be annoying. It got so bad she filed a restraining order against him.

"My daughter has been missing for six weeks from the Puyallup Fair," Diana wrote in the restraining order. "Cory Bober has called me on a daily basis, telling me my daughter is dead. I was advised by Deputy Brian Coburn to file this complaint if I felt threatened."

The order would only last two weeks. Diana would then call the courts and rescind her request. She would later call Bober and apologize. Her daughter had been missing for over 56 days. Bober was annoying as hell but he was the only one doing research. The only one who cared.

Bober organized a volunteer search for Misty in the Green River area. He somehow coerced someone on the police forensic team to tell him the general vicinity of where one of the Puyallup girl's body was found. Bober surmised that Misty's body would be found in the same general area.

Seventy-two days after Misty had gone missing, there was now a volunteer team searching for her.

Nothing came out of the search.

But Diana would later spot Rheuban at a grocery store and confront him. The young man ran and got into a truck with an older man. She saw the look of fear and apprehension on both men as they sped off.

Diana would then lapse into a depression. She tried to commit suicide with booze and prescription drugs.

The next day she would wake up in a hospital. She would spend the next day there, drying out until being discharged back into the nightmare that had become her life.

A PLEA TO THE PUBLIC

Four months after Misty's disappearance, Diana would appear on a local TV station for a special on the Green River Killer. Jim Doyon, the homicide detective who worked the case, spoke of the killings but deferred on stating if Delange and Chebetnoy(the slain Puyallup girls) were connected.

Doyon took an interest in Misty's case. He would journey to Highway 410 and search near milepost 30 where the bodies of Delange and Chebetnoy had been discovered.

Like Bober and the volunteer search team, he too came up empty.

Bober was undaunted and organized another search. He realized that they had been searching in the wrong spot. They were searching on the south side of the highway when the should have been searching on the north.

Twelve people would show up for the search. Diana would arrive with her older sister, Debra. Bober would arrive with Al Hensley, the father of one of the slain Puyallup girls along with his 14-year old Boy Scout nephew, Jaremy Brown.

It would be the Boy Scout that would make the find

Poking into a ditch with his stick, he saw the crumpled blue jeans. Socks fell out of the jeans.

Baggy and stone-washed, they were cuffed at the bottom. The same jeans that Misty had borrowed from her mother on the night of the fair. The jeans were too big for her and Diana remembered them cuffing them on the bottom.

Bober became excited. He knew that the killer had planted the jeans there as a taunt.

He was right. The police were wrong.

But Diana, according to her sister, "broke into a million pieces."

THE KILLING FIELD

Seven dead women had been found in the nine-mile stretch between Enumclaw and Greenwater in the eight years prior to Misty's disappearance.

The two slain Puyallup girls were found in the same area in 1988 and 1991, only one hundred feet apart. They were left off a footpath that had been hidden by thick brush.

Both of the teenage girls had been presumed abducted from the Puyallup shopping center. Detective Jim Doyon believed privately that the cases were connected. He arrived at the site where Misty's jeans were found and interviewed witnesses, particularly Diana and Bober.

The jeans were taken to the lab and the forensic analysis indicated that the jeans had been in the ditch for some time.

Police suspected that someone (Bober? Diana?) had planted the jeans there.

What was undeniable that the jeans were found only a ten minute walk away from where the bodies of the two slain Puyallup girls were found.

SUSPICIONS ARISE

People began to talk. There were reporters who believed the jeans were planted there. Some were talking as if Diana and Bober were lovers and had plotted this for some insurance money.

Dede Miles, a fifteen-year-old friend of Misty, would come to Sgt. Carver with a tip. She said there was a boy that kept coming over to Misty's parties. He would always leave before her mother came home.

His name was Rheuban Schmidt.

Finally, the unkempt looking young man would come under the radar of the police.

Diana, meanwhile, began to suspect Cory Bober.

How did he know where to look? Why was this stranger so interested in the case to begin with? How did he know so much?

The police had warned her to stay away from him. Now she felt compelled to tell the police of her suspicions.

"Diana comes to station. Now feels Cory Bober may be involved in Misty's disappearance. I asked Diana to submit a written statement to that effect and why she feels he may be involved – she agreed to do so."

Carver's notes

AN INTERVIEW WITH TRINA

Detective Jim Doyon would interview the fifteen-year-old Trina Bevard, the last person to see Misty alive.

Six months had passed. Doyon had brought along the jeans with him, the sight of which made Trina cry.

"It seems to me like something that Misty was wearing that night," Trina said. "It looks very close to what Misty was wearing. The socks, they match what she was wearing. The jeans are big, so – her jeans were baggy that night, that she was wearing. They're – they were light blue like they are in the photo. It just seems, you know, it was the clothes that she was wearing."

Doyon would go on to ask what she was wearing (a pullover) and if she had any jewelry. He then asked if she had any cigarettes or birth control pills.

"No," Trina said. "She was straight. She was a virgin. She didn't smoke, she didn't drink, she didn't do drugs. She was clean, so she had no reason to do anything. She wasn't sexually active."

Trina then revealed that the girls made five calls to Rheuban. They could not get a hold of him. They finally got him on the line and he still refused to pick them up even when the girls offered him money. Misty told him about a key under the front doormat of her home. He could go inside, get money for gas and come pick them up.

Trina stated that she didn't trust Rheuban but only because he didn't keep his word and come pick them up. She then called a 23-year old friend named Mike Rhyner for a ride but they got disconnected. The girls were then stranded. They walked downtown to get to the bus stop before spotting a phone booth by a convenience store. Misty then called her mother, telling her that if Rheuban didn't come pick her up she would take the bus. The two argued as Diana didn't want Misty around Rheuban.

Trina had to get home by 10 p.m. She had about an hour and a half to get home which wasn't that far. Misty could not walk the ten miles to Spanaway.

Trina then decided to walk. She gave Misty her extra money for the bus.

"At that time I made my decision of walking home and she said she would take the bus," Trina recalled. "The last words that I said to her were 'Be careful,' and she turned around and told me the same and we walked off in different directions"

Trina also dismissed the notion of Misty being a runaway.

" Her mom just bought her a stereo and she was so excited and she went shopping and she got new clothes,"Trina recalled. She was telling me all about it. She was really excited about it.

BOBER GOES TO JAIL

Meanwhile, Bober would be sentenced to fourteen months in prison for the marijuana possession. He felt that the sentencing was too punitive and threatened law enforcement that they would never find Misty without him. His fellow inmates thought he was crazy and began calling him "snitch" and "The Green River Killer".

Jail would not slow down Bober's efforts, however. He continued to research and write Misty's mother.

"Dear Diana,

...When we found Misty's clothes, part of me died and I watched a part of you die too (much more than a "part") and I was at a total loss for words. I never wanted to be the one to show you your most horrible fears were true and that your daughter is truly dead at the hands of a sick murderer. I will never rest until the killer (Randy Achziger) is brought to justice and dead, if it takes my life to do it."

AMERICA'S MOST WANTED

Misty's case would eventually be broadcast nationally as it was featured on the America's Most Wanted television show.

Over twenty-eight tips came into Sgt. Carver from people who watched the broadcast.

When the tips went nowhere, Diana's suspicions returned to her original suspect, Rheuban Schmidt. She wanted Carver to speak to the young man but the Sergeant would take a circuitous route to get to Schmidt.

Carver would speak to Frank Rodriguez, the owner of Adam's Ribs, a restaurant where Rheuban worked. He convinced the owner to try and find out how much Rheuban knew about Misty.

"3-4-93 @ 1500: Frank states Rheuban said the following during a lengthy conversation about Misty Copsey:
- Yeah, I know about it.
- I know exactly where she is buried.
- They found the clothes but she is buried 6 miles from there.
- They're off by 6 or 6 1/2 miles."
— Excerpt from Carver's notes

Carver would then wait for Rheuban outside the restaurant before his shift started. Schmidt arrived, saw the cops and immediately ran off. The detectives would eventually catch up with him.

Rheuban would concede that he had received calls from Misty the night of her disappearance. But his story corroborated with Trina's, he told the girls he had no gas and could not pick them up.

Carver then asked if he knew where Misty was buried but Rheuban was adamant that he "said those things to get Frank off my back."

Rheuban then revealed that he suffered from "black outs". He stated that he did not recall anything until the daylight hours of September 18th, 1992.

The detectives pounced, asking if it was possible that he blacked out, picked up Misty and harmed her.

Rheuban claimed he didn't know.

All he knew was that he drove out to his grandmother's farmhouse and couldn't recall why.

Detectives would then give Rheuban a polygraph test.

They would later state that the suspect "zoned out" during the test, nearly falling asleep. The tests were inconclusive but detectives felt as if he were trying to beat the test.

A LITTLE LIE

Rheuban fell off the detective's radar when Carver talked to Dede Miles again. Dede would tell the detective that Trina had not walked home from the fairground like she told him.

Dede said that Trina had a boyfriend come pick her up and didn't want anyone to know.

Trina's boyfriend's name was Michael J. Rhyner. He had nothing on his record aside from traffic stops but he had friends that were connected with Chebetnoy and Delange.

He also had a complaint when he was sixteen years old. He was accused of an abduction rape wherein he used a knife and a cigarette lighter to terrorize an eleven-year-old.

Charges were never filed for an undisclosed reason.

Carver brought Trina in for more questioning. He wanted the truth. The truth about who picked her up that night. The truth about Misty.

But the truth was that Trina told the Sgt. Carver and Detective Tom Matison that she lied because she feared "getting into trouble with her guardian about it."

Trina admitted that she called Rhyner, got disconnected and left a message. She told Misty that they could both ride with Rhyner but Misty said no.

"Trina would not be specific why Misty did not trust Rhyner, but the indication was that Rhyner might have 'come on' to Misty at one time and she did not like it. Trina states that she and Rhyner are friends, but not involved."

— Matison's notes

Trina said that she started to walk and then Rhyner picked her up and dropped her off. The detectives asked if perhaps Rhyner had picked up Misty but she said no.

FRANK RODRIGUEZ' FOLLOW UP

Diana would state that Frank Rodriguez, Rheuban's employer, would call her to say that Rheuban had "bragged about doing something" to Misty with his uncle. Frank didn't fully believe him, however, as Rheuban was "weird" and always bragging about stuff he didn't do.

Diana then approached Carver about Rheuban and the sergeant went ballistic.

"We have our man!" he said.

The man he sought was Michael Rhyner, Trina Bevard's boyfriend.

"We share our knowledge of Mike Rhyner and how he is involved with Misty and Trina – and the fact Trina lied to Doyon. We state that there is an excellent possibility that Rhyner may be linked to Chebetnoy and DeLange. Exchange of information is extremely beneficial."

— Carver's notes

"Sgt. Carver believes that Rhyner dropped Bevard off, returned to the area of the fairgrounds, located Misty Copsey, convinced her to get into his vehicle and drove off with her."

— Doyon's notes

Police set up a sting on Rhyner. The car mechanic was selling his 1981 blue Ford Escort for $200 bucks.

The buyer was an undercover cop.

He watched as Rhyner hurriedly took out trash from the car before the sale. The police then did a forensic examination of the car.

Meanwhile, Rheuban's green Nova was being crushed at a wrecking yard. The Puyallup police didn't care as the tweaker was no longer on their radar. Also, Randy Achziger, Bober's suspect, had been charged and convicted for the rape of a seven-year-old.

INTERROGATING RHYNER

Ideally, Detectives Matison and Sgt. Carver wanted the forensics back from Rhyner's Escort before they spoke to him. But the wait became interminable and they brought him in for questioning without some evidence to back up their suspicions.

Rhyner's story would match that of Trina's. He picked Trina up and went back home. He said that he and Trina were only "good friends" and he had met Misty only four times. Matison then asked Rhyner if he felt Misty was alive and what should happen to the person who harmed her.

Rhyner knew what the detective was getting at. On his own volition, Rhyner told the detectives about his juvenile complaint from years ago. He stated he had been cleared and knew that was why they were looking at him now.

"First thing I thought, you know, well, that's in my file," Rhyner said. "Now you guys are going to think I did it since it's in my file. About Misty, that's the one thing that worried me."

Rhyner then passed a polygraph test.

Grasping at straws, the police then turned their sights back on Rheuban. If only they had impounded his car when they had the chance...

TOO LITTLE TOO LATE

"Rheuban Schmidt's initial interview with Sgt. Carver and I created more questions than answers. He was very vague about what he did that September 17th and finally said that he had a 'blackout' and 'woke up' at his grandmother's property near Enumclaw.

...Schmidt had told Frank Rodriguez that Misty's body was six miles from where the jeans were found. He now claims that he said this just to get Rodriguez "off his back," and was not a true statement.

He was driving a Green Chev Nova at the time but he no longer has the vehicle. It was repossessed.

Schmidt also mentioned that his Grandmother's property is located in King County by Buckley and is over a hundred acres. The property has cows on it. Few people enter onto the property."

— Matison's notes

Tinsley, fifteen years old at the time of Misty's disappearance, told police the Rheuban was his roommate for only a few months. He described Rheuban as a short-tempered guy who had a thirteen-year-old girlfriend. The girlfriend, Tinsley said, got jealous when Rheuban got a call from Misty.

Tinsley stated that Rheuban had left the apartment in a huff then came back between eleven and one at night.

So Rheuban did not "black out" as he told detectives. N

"What do you think might have happened to her?" Matison asked.

"Um, I couldn't, I couldn't say because I have no idea," Tinsley said.

"Well, can you speculate?"

"With Rheuban, this is just that I, this, this is what I say with Rheuban because I, I figure that um that he, he tried to, he tried to um, get with her or something and she said, she said no and he got all pissed and did something, I don't know, that's just a second guess."

"You think Rheuban would be capable of ah, kidnapping and killing somebody?"

"I think he could," Tinsley said.

Detectives would meet with Rheuban again, relaying the information that Tinsley recalled him coming back to the apartment that night.

But Rheuban remained adamant in stating that he didn't remember what he did. The detectives then drove him out to his grandmother's farm which had over 100-acres...100 secluded acres.

Detective Matison would note that Rheuban's grandmother's house six miles north of Buckley. Rheuban told Frank that Misty would be buried six miles away from where her jeans were found which would place it in the close vicinity of his grandmother's farm. They would go to inquire with his grandmother but she was not home.

They did not follow-up with the grandmother .

Even so, Rheuban's story no longer held up. He told Misty that he didn't have any gas. He lived sixteen miles away from the fair.

But then he stated that he had driven to his grandmother's farm in Buckley then returned home.

A sixty-mile round trip.

Detectives would give him another polygraph test which he passed.

"It appears that Rheuban Schmidt was not involved in the disappearance of Misty Copsey. He, however, has no alibi as to his movements during the evening of her disappearance, as well as no memory; he claimed that he had a blackout. He acknowledges that he left the residence of James Tinsley, but does not remember what he did.

Investigation to continue."

— Matison's notes

ONE YEAR ANNIVERSARY

The local media ran a few more stories on Misty's disappearance as the Puyallup Fair started. The forensic test on Rhyner's test finally came through. There was no match with Misty anywhere.

Now once again grasping at straws, Carver would turn to Diana and her associates. He would interview Diana's parole officer and one of her ex-boyfriends.

Misty's father, Buck, was asked to take a polygraph test. He gave consent and passed.

"I explained to her that missing person investigations, at some point in time, must eliminate the parents of any wrongdoing. Diana agreed to the examination."

— Carver's notes

Diana would pass her polygraph test but Jim Corey, Doyon's colleague, said that Diana's polygraph would prove to be inconclusive and that perhaps she had something to do with planting the jeans at the location on Hwy 410.

Carver had always had his doubts about Diana and felt that she planted the jeans.

But the leads would eventually dry up. After nine years, Misty Copsey's disappearance would turn cold.

No one was ever charged with her disappearance.

THE AFTERMATH

Diana would hand out fliers at the Puyallup Fairgrounds every year.

She was doing more than law enforcement and even the media.

Every now and then, a local reporter would run a story about Misty. A few cranks would call in and say that they knew something but it would lead to nowhere. Then that would be it. Everything would run dry.

Detective Jim Doyon felt that she was deceased.

BOBER TO THE RESCUE

Bober was then caught for marijuana possession again but this time, he pressed for an advantage. He would gain the Washington State Patrol crime lab report on Misty's jeans, compiled after their 1993 discovery.

He argued that the lab report was part of his defense....he gambled and won.

Obtaining the prized document, the amateur sleuth went to work. The report stated there was no blood, no semen. But there were hairs, fibers, and three red paint chips. There were also holes in the left leg in the jeans, above the knee.

Bober knew that somehow, someway, Randy Achziger was involved. That he killed Misty.

The forensic details raced through Bober's head...red paint chips...red paint chips...

He knew that Bober had a red Porsche. He knew that the paint chips would match.

But the police had another suspect they didn't tell anyone about.

Robert Leslie Hickey.

Hickey's hunting ground was the Puyallup area where he specialized in abduction rapes.

He also drove a red Camaro.

Puyallup police had him on their list as a possible suspect but he was never questioned nor did they obtain forensic samples from his car.

Thirteen years later, however, they would collect samples from Achziger's old car. The car had been sold and the new owner was open to having forensics performed on it.

The particles would be sent to a crime lab which already had a backlog of over a year.

With nothing else left to do, the police turned once again to Rheuban Schmidt.

"I think it's worth taking another shot at Schmidt, and we're planning on it. He's been clean since 1993 ...

— Excerpt from notes by Lt. Dave McDonald, March 19, 2006

Only Schmidt had not been clean. He had been convicted of second-degree theft in 2000. In early 1996, he was accused of rape by one of Misty's best friends. He had held a pillow over her face to silence her but two weeks after filing the report, the girl back away from her accusation and did not file charges.

"[She] told me that she would be undergoing counseling related to the rape, but that she did not want to undergo any additional stress that may be caused by further investigation or possible prosecution in this matter.

Case cleared exceptional/refused by victim."

— Pierce County sheriff's report, Feb. 6, 1996

Later in 2006, Puyallup police gathered more reports on Rheuban. One was a domestic violence protection order requested by his wife, the mother of his three children.

"Rheuban has previously told her that if she ever had him served with a court order he'd 1) burn her house down with her and her kids in it, and 2) send 'some guys' to kick in her door and take money from her.

(She) said Rheuban told her that they'd get money from her if they had to beat her, rape her and then rob her.

(She) said Rheuban told her that if it came to that she 'wouldn't be breathing' when they were done with her."

— Pierce County Sheriff's report, Nov. 9, 2006

MISSING PAINT CHIPS

Adding more incompetence to the investigation, the red paint chips found on Misty's jeans would turn up "missing." All that remained inside the bag where the chips were marked was a piece of plastic.

The lab technicians now had no way to match the red chips on Misty's jeans to Achziger's red Porsche.

Bober would claim that the red chips did match and the police were now trying to save face. Diana, however, no longer wants anything to do with him.

Bober would state that the police would tell Diana that they had, in fact, tested the red paint found on Misty's clothes against Achziger's Porsche. Bober discovered that the red paint was missing beforehand yet the police would lie to Diana about the test.

The lies and incompetence that began investigation have seemingly ended it as well. The Puyallup police relied far too heavily on polygraph tests to discount suspects where their own accounts (particularly in the case of Schmidt) were shaky at best. They failed to secure possession of Schmidt's Green Nova which may have proven to provide forensic evidence that Misty was in his vehicle.

Twenty-four years have elapsed since Misty's disappearance.

Her case remains unsolved.

9 798224 763146